Lewis and Clark

Discover The Life Of An Explorer

Trish Kline

Rourke Publishing LLC
Vero Beach, Florida 32964

PHOTO CREDITS:
©Charles Saint-M*min/Wood River Gallery; ©Getty Images: title page, pages 7, 17; ©Archive Photos: cover; ©Phyllis Picardi/Stock Boston, Inc: page 10; ©Andre Jenny/Focus Group: page 12; ©Artville LLC: page 13; ©James P. Rowan: pages 15, 18; Library of Congress: pages 9, 21

EDITORIAL SERVICES:
Pamela Schroeder

Library of Congress Cataloging-in-Publication Data

Kline, Trish.
    Lewis and Clark / Trish Kline.
        p. cm. — (Discover the life of an explorer)
    Includes bibliographical references and index.
    ISBN 1-58952-067-X
    1. Lewis, Meriwether, 1744-1809—Juvenile literature. 2. Clark, William, 1770-1838—Juvenile literature. 3. Explorers—West (U.S.)—Biography—Juvenile literature. 4. Lewis and Clark Expedition (1804-1806)—Juvenile literature. 5. West (U.S.)—Discovery and exploration—Juvenile literature. [Lewis, Meriwether, 1774-1809. 2. Clark, William, 1770-1838. 3. Lewis and Clark Expedition (1804-1806) 4. Explorers. 5. West (U.S.)—Discovery and exploration.] I. Title.

F592.7 .K59 2001
917.804'2'0922—dc21   2001019001

Printed in the USA

TABLE OF CONTENTS

TWO YOUTHS

Meriwether Lewis was born in 1774. He grew up in Virginia. His family owned a big farm. Lewis went to school. He learned to read and write. He enjoyed learning about nature. He liked to draw pictures of plants.

William Clark was born in 1770 in Kentucky. Clark did not go to school. His older brother taught him about reading, writing, and nature. Clark learned about animals and plants. He learned to hunt and live in the wild.

Meriwether Lewis loved nature and grew up to become an explorer.

TWO SOLDIERS

In 1789 William Clark joined the U.S. Army. He built forts. He led soldiers. He also learned to draw maps. He became a captain.

In 1795 a soldier named Meriwether Lewis was sent to Captain William Clark. The men became good friends. Both were good leaders.

Captain William Clark became good friends with Meriwether Lewis.

A PRESIDENT CALLS

In 1801 Thomas Jefferson became President of the United States. He asked Meriwether Lewis to be his **secretary**.

In 1803 President Jefferson wanted to send **explorers** to the West. President Jefferson needed a leader who could do the job. He asked Lewis. Lewis wrote to his old friend William Clark. He asked Clark to be a leader, too.

President Thomas Jefferson hired Lewis and Clark to explore the West.

THE MISSION

In 1803 very few people lived west of the Mississippi River. President Jefferson knew settlers would not decide to move there easily. No one knew what the land was like. There were no maps to help settlers know where they should build homes.

Lewis and Clark's mission was simple. Go west. Keep **journals**. Write about everything. Write about the land, the animals, and the plants. Write about the Native American tribes and draw maps.

Lewis and Clark made maps and wrote about their travels.

A Lewis and Clark monument overlooks Council Bluffs in Iowa.

This map shows the path of Lewis and Clark.

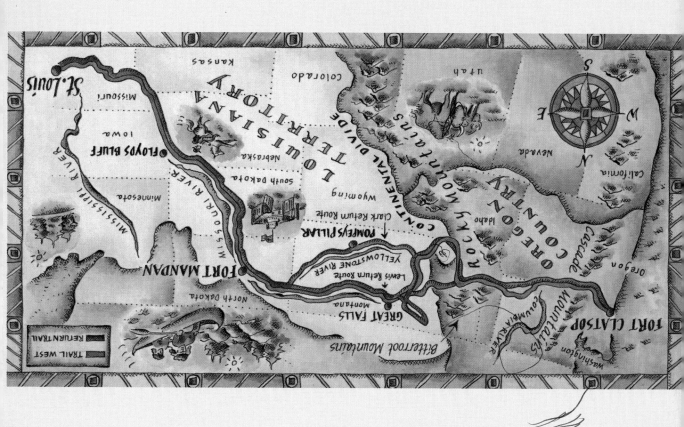

HELP ALONG THE WAY

The trip west took almost four years. Lewis and Clark traveled many miles. They went up rivers by boat. They crossed prairies and mountains. The summers were dry and dusty. The winters were very cold and snowy.

*Lewis and Clark traveled the
Missouri River by boat.*

They met many tribes of Native Americans. The Native Americans often helped Lewis and Clark. A Native American woman named *Sacagawea* traveled with Lewis and Clark. She helped them understand the **language** of Native American tribes. She also helped Lewis and Clark trade for horses and food.

Sacagawea helped Lewis and Clark trade with Native Americans.

WELCOME HOME, HEROES!

In the fall of 1806, their trip was finished. Lewis and Clark had crossed many miles of land. The lands they crossed would soon become new states. These new states would be Kansas, Nebraska, South Dakota, North Dakota, Montana, Idaho, Oregon, and Washington.

Lewis and Clark built Fort Clatsop when they reached Oregon.

SETTLERS FOLLOW THE TRAIL

Meriwether Lewis was named governor of the Louisiana **Territory**. He died in 1809. He was 35 years old.

William Clark became a general. He was also named as governor of the Missouri Territory. For many years, people brought him news about the West. He used this news to draw new maps. He died in 1838 at age 68.

Meriwether Lewis was named governor of the Louisiana Territory.

IMPORTANT DATES TO REMEMBER

1770   William Clark was born.

1774   Meriwether Lewis was born.

1795   Lewis and Clark met and became friends.

1803   President Jefferson sent Lewis and Clark out west to explore.

1806   Lewis and Clark returned to Washington. Meriwether Lewis became governor of the Louisiana Territory.

1809   Lewis died at age 35.

1813   Clark became governor of the Missouri Territory.

1838   Clark died at age 68.

GLOSSARY

explorers (ik SPLOR erz) — people who travel to unknown places

journals (JUR nalz) — written records of day-to-day events

language (LANG gwij) — words spoken by a tribe or other related group of people

secretary (SEK ri ter ee) — a person who is hired to write letters and other papers

territory (TER i tor ee) — an area of land

INDEX

Further Reading

Sawyer, Bonnie Sachatello. *Lewis and Clark.* Scholastic, 1997.
Twist, Clint. *Lewis and Clark: Exploring the Northwest.* Raintree Steck-Vaughn, 1994.
Roop, Peter. *The Journals of Lewis and Clark.* Walker & Company, 1993.

Websites To Visit

www.pbs.org
www.encarta.msn.com

About The Author

Trish Kline is a seasoned curriculum writer. She has written a great number of nonfiction books for the school and library market. Her print publishing credits include two dozen books as well as hundreds of newspaper and magazine articles, anthologies, short stories, poetry, and plays. She currently resides in Helena, Montana.

Pen noted
7/2020 SMF